NO HANG-UPS II

CLIFF CARLE

Illustrated by Greg Tenorio

CCC Publications • Los Angeles

Published by

CCC Publications
20306 Tau Place
Chatsworth, CA 91311

Copyright © 1986 Cliff Carle

Manufactured in the United States of America

Cover design & illustrations © 1986 CCC Publications

ISBN: 0-918259-05-3

First CCC Publications printing — July 1986

If your local bookstore is out of stock, copies of this book may be obtained by mailing a check or money order for $3.95 per book (plus $1.00 to cover sales tax, postage, and handling) to: CCC Publications/20306 Tau Pl., Chatsworth, CA 91311.

*CONTRIBUTORS

Twyla Ahre, Geralyn Ashum, Fred Baker, John Beckman, Harold Capps, Sandy Conroy, Dustin Drew, Cynthia Fena, Andrea Fitz, Janine Gates, Patricia Gaynor, Doug Grimes, Barbara Harrell, Marti Harrell, Nancy Higgins, Margaret Highley, Rick Hornburg, Gary Kubina, Bobbie Lavender & Cathy Door, Ron LaVigne, Amy Lewis, Patricia Lindsey, Denruth Lougeay, Joseph Marraffa, Loni Marsten, Michele Maggio, M. M. McKay & F. B. McKay, Linda Morales, K. W. Morimoto, Randall & Janice Petersen, Bill Pollanger, Rainbow, J. J. Ramberg & Anita Banchik, Marina Ritz, Richard Rogers, Katy Rosolowski, John Schwartz, Robert Schwarz, Celeste Simich, Lainie Sorkin, G. E. Terry, Ena & Angela Valikov, Denise Van Ravenstein, Connie Ward.

A special thanks to everyone who sent in a "Richer & Famous" coupon from the first book. Due to space limitations, we were only able to use but a few of the many funny and clever submissions we received.

To those of you whose messages did not appear in this book, and to anyone who submits future "R. & F." coupons, we would like you to know that your message may be used in NO HANG-UPS III.

*Asterisks throughout the book denote contributed messages

CONTENTS

INTRODUCTION

Welcome to my second book of funny and clever answering machine messages!

I first want to thank the "multitudes" out there who made the first book a national bestseller—thus giving me the green light for this sequel.

Over the past year, I received "tons" of mail from many concerned answering machine owners (and a few "carefree" machine owners). Along with some very flattering accolades, the letters contained numerous suggestions for NO HANG-UPS II. Of course, I ignored them all. It is merely a *coincidence* that a lot of people asked, "How about some messages for *two* people who share a machine?"—and I just happen to have a chapter for "Roommates & Couples." Other people asked, "How about some very short messages (under 15 seconds) for machines with a limited outgoing tape?"—and so what if I also have a chapter entitled, "Short & Sour"?

But seriously, folks, your many comments were very helpful in both the writing and 'chapterization' of this new batch of messages. Thanks!

INSTRUCTIONS: As in the first book, I have used arbitrary names ("JAN" and "JOE") and the surname "DOE". With a few exceptions, most messages will work for either a male or female by simply inserting your own name and/or switching the gender of the pronouns (e.g. "he" to "she").

On some messages, I've omitted the standard line, "leave your name, your number and a message. . ." because, by now, almost everyone has reached a machine and knows what is expected of them after the beep.

Also, from some of the mail, it appears that certain people are under the impression that to alter in any way the wording of a printed message is *illegal*. Please, by any and all means, edit or personalize or reword these messages till your pencil runs out of lead (which, personally, I've *never* seen happen). You have my word the *Answering Machine Police* won't come knocking on your door with a warrant for "message tampering"!

Whatever you do, be sure of one thing—and this is what NO HANG-UPS II is all about— have fun!

—Cliff Carle

P.S. I hope each and every one of you enters CCC Publications' contest for the best message. Since it has nothing to do with luck, I wish you all good *skill*!

PHONEY EXCUSES

Hi. JOE here. We had a pretty wild party last night, so I'm sleepin' in. I gotta tell ya, some people are so rude! The neighbor below us was poundin' on his ceiling all night! We hadda keep turning the stereo up to drown him out!

BEEP. . .

Hi. It's my day off and I decided that today I'm going to do *absolutely nothing*. Leave a message and I'll call back when I'm finished.

BEEP. . .

Hi. Sorry I can't pick up the phone. I'll be studying all night. I wanna be sure and get an "A" on my urine test tomorrow!

BEEP. . .

Hi. I'm home, but won't be picking up the phone. It's my lunchtime, so I'm relaxing here and having some Alphabet Soup. But, I should be able to get back to you soon—I'm already up to the "M's".

BEEP. . .

*

Hello. This is JOE. I can't come to the phone. I'm at the Police Station. There seems to be a mix-up here. I was at the grocery store a couple of hours ago and I saw this sign that said, "Pepsi Free", so I took a six-pack and left. Oh well, leave a name and number. . .

BEEP. . .

(LOW VOICE)
Yo. I think I'm being followed. I know they're on to me, so I'd better speak in code:
Leave your ame-nay and umber-nay at the one-tay!
(WHISPER)
And don't forget to wipe your fingerprints off your receiver!

BEEP. . .

*
(SNOBBY VOICE)
Hello. There is no one available to accept your call at this time. The maid is upstairs dusting, and since the chauffeur quit, the butler is out waxing the Rolls Royce. You just can't find good help these days!

BEEP. . .

*
Hello. This is JOE's machine. Thanks to a merciless ex-wife, JOE is down on the corner in his shabby clothes with a tin cup. Leave a message at the tone and just as soon as he can beg a quarter, he'll return your call.

BEEP. . .

4

Hi. It's my lunchtime, so you'll have to leave a message. You know, I gotta say I'm kinda proud of myself 'cuz lately I've been careful about what I eat. Like, I've really cut down on salt—now I only have it with my meals!

BEEP. . .

Hi. Leave a message. As usual, I'll be browsing around at the bookstore. Yesterday I almost bought this new dictionary—but I think I'm gonna wait until the movie comes out.

BEEP. . .

Hi. Please leave a message. I'm outside working on my tan. I tell ya, I really love tanning! I could lay out in the sun day and night!

BEEP. . .

(EXCITED)
Hi. I'm going over to my new girlfriend's. Yesterday, I gave her a rose and she kissed me. So today, I'm giving her two dozen!

BEEP. . .

*

BIRTHDAY

Hello. Today is JOE's birthday—which makes him one year older and a little more slower. So, if he can't get to the phone in time, have a heart and leave a message.

BEEP. . .

Hi. Please leave your number, even if I already have it in my address book. I can't see a thing without my glasses, which I lost and can't look for until I find where I put 'em.

BEEP. . .

(SNOBBISH UPPER CLASS / OR "HICK" ATTITUDE)
Good day. We're truly sorry you missed us, but we're off on another European vacation—first class, of course. You know, last month we went to Venice, Italy and just our luck—the trip cost over ten grand and when we got there, the whole place was flooded!

BEEP. . .

*

Hi. This is JAN. I'm in the bath tub right now with (*YOUR FAVORITE STAR*). But leave a message and I'll get back to you— if the water ever gets cold!

BEEP. . .

Hi. This is JAN. I had to go to the doctor. I think I'm losing my mind! Everytime I ask someone what time it is, I get a different answer!

BEEP. . .

Hi. I'm not home. I'm out on a date with this real *sexy* librarian—when she reads, she moves her *hips*.

BEEP. . .

*

Hi. This is Rover, the DOE family's dog. They're all taking a shower together to conserve energy. You could give your message to me, but since I'm illiterate, you better leave it on this machine.

BEEP. . .

*

Hi. This is JAN. Please leave a message. I went over to my neighbor's house to give him some ice cubes. He ran out and, unfortunately, he lost the recipe.

BEEP. . .

Hi. This is JOE. Sorry you missed me this morning, but I ran out of gas as I got home last night—so I had to get up extra early this morning and go to a filling station. Boy, I sure hope it doesn't hurt my car to drive on an empty tank!

BEEP. . .

*

Hi. I can't take your call right now, 'cuz I'm teaching my pet goldfish how to talk. But leave your name and number and either he or I will get back to you.
(ASIDE)
Okay, say "Guppy wanna cracker!"

BEEP. . .

Hi. This is JAN. I'll be out for a while. The bank returned a check of mine, so I'm gonna go out and buy some more with it!

BEEP. . .

XMAS MESSAGE

(FLUSTERED)
Hi. I've gone to the Mall and I'll probably be there all day! Boy, can anybody tell me why Christmas always comes when the stores are so crowded!?!

BEEP. . .

Hi. I can't come to the phone. I recently signed up for one of those esoteric University Extension Courses called, "Drawing On The Right Side Of The Brain." So, I'm in the bathroom shaving my head.

BEEP. . .

Hi. Sorry if you left a message and I didn't get back to you right away. What happened was, I was driving last week and came to a sign that said, *"Road Closed During Construction."* So I had to park and wait for them to finish.

BEEP...

*
(STUFFY)
Hello. This is the DOE residence; James, the family butler, speaking. The DOE family is out picking cotton and slopping the hogs. Leave a message and they will return your call. Thank you.

BEEP...

(RUSHED)
Hi. Please leave a message. My great uncle had an emergency—his wooden leg developed termites, so I had to rush him to a tree surgeon!

BEEP...

(WASTED)
Well... It was another wild night! *Wine, women* and *song* are doing me in! No doubt about it, I'm going to have to give up *singing*!

BEEP...

ROOMMATES & COUPLES

(FAST)

A Hello! You've reached the *Telephone Answering Machine Game Show*, where callers get a chance to win fabulous prizes. This is JOE. . .

B And JAN!

A We're your co-hosts! Tell them how it works, JAN!

B When you hear the tone, if you are able to identify yourself and correctly tell us the digits of your telephone number, you will win a luxurious and exciting return call from JOE and JAN!

A Thank you, JAN! And now, here's our first contestant:

BEEP. . .

(OPEN AND SHUT DRAWERS)

A Maybe it's in *this* drawer?

B (MAD)
I already looked in that drawer!

A Well, why didn't you *tell* me!

B I *just* did! Look in that other drawer!

A Don't be silly. It wouldn't be in there!

B Oh, hi. Excuse us, we're looking for our marriage license. . .

A We want to see what the expiration date is. . .

BEEP. . .

A (GRAND VOICE)
And now... the moment you've all been waiting for...

B (NORMAL VOICE)
JOE AND JAN have a new message...

BEEP...

(IN BACKGROUND, HAVE WATER RUNNING AND ROOMMATE OR SPOUSE **A** SINGING OFF-KEY)

B Hi. We can't come to the phone. My roommate is in the shower and I'll be outside where the neighbors can see me—I don't want them to think I'm torturing the cat!

BEEP...

17

A (MALE VOICE)
Hi. I'm heading off to work and my wife is going shopping as soon as she finishes making my lunch.
(CONFIDENTIAL TONE)
You know, maybe I'm just a little paranoid, but lately, I've been getting the feeling my wife wants to get rid of me...

B (FEMALE VOICE—UNEMOTIONAL)
Here's your lunch, JOE.

A (MALE VOICE)
Thanks, JAN. Uh, I see you wrapped it in a road map again...

BEEP...

A Okay, JOE, it's your turn to record the message.

B I don't feel like it, JAN. Why don't you do it today?

A I do it *every* day! You always put it off—you're such a procrastinator!

B A What?

A Procrastinator! You know what procrastination is?

B I was gonna look that word up once, but I never got around to it.

BEEP. . .

A (SNORING)

B (WHISPERING)
Shhhhhhhhh! Hi. Leave a message, but please do it quietly. My roommate just got home from his therapist's and now he's doing his homework.

BEEP. . .

A JOE, I can name that tune in three notes!

B JAN, I can name that tune in two notes!

A JOE, I can name that tune in one note!

B Okay, JAN, here's your *one* note:

BEEP. . .

A (MALE VOICE)
Hi. This is JOE. *Ouch*! I'll be taking off. . . *Ouch*! as soon as I finish shaving here. . . *Ouch*! and JAN is working down in the basement. . . *Ouch*! so you'll have to leave a message. . . *Ouch*!

B (FEMALE VOICE—IN BACKGROUND)
JOE? Where's your razor? I need it again to finish scraping the old varnish off this table!

BEEP. . .

A How about if I *sing* a message today?

B No way!

A C'mon, everybody says I have a rich voice.

B Well, why don't you retire it!

A When I sing, people clap their hands.

B Over their ears!

A C'mon, don't you think I sing with feeling?

B I think if you had any feelings, you wouldn't sing!

A (SINGS)
"Leave a message at the sound of the tone!"

B (SINGS)
"Another note and you'll be living alone!"

BEEP...

SHORT & SOUR

Hi. This is JAN. At the sound of the message, please leave a tone.

BEEP...

*
You've reached JOE's machine. This message is like men's underwear. . . brief.

BEEP. . .

Hi. I had to go see my lawyer. He's one of the best there is—got his training in Iowa—*Sioux City*!

BEEP. . .

*
The Human is gone,
I'm just a machine.
Here goes the beep,
You know the routine. . .

BEEP. . .

Hi. This is Mary. I'm going out to dinner. I think I'll have a little lamb. . .

BEEP. . .

(FAST)
This JAN—not home—leave message—call back!

BEEP. . .

(IRISH ACCENT)
Hello. You've reached *Dial-A-Confession*. At the tone, please leave your name, number and a brief sin. . .

BEEP. . .

*

Hi. Do you remember the days of nickel beer, dime cigars, and 25 cent gasoline? Well, those days are gone and so am I!

BEEP. . .

(HAVE SOMEONE OF THE OPPOSITE SEX RECORD THIS MESSAGE FOR YOU:)
Hi. This is JOE/JAN. I'm sorry if it doesn't sound like me, but I'm not feeling myself today.

BEEP. . .

Hi. This is JOE. I'm feelin' great! I went to a mind reader today and only got charged half price!

BEEP. . .

26

*

This is the DOE Summer Home.
Summer home and *summer* not!

BEEP. . .

Hello. You have reached *Le' Machine*.
If you leave *le' message*,
I'll call you *le' back*.

BEEP. . .

*

Yeah, yeah, I know! Another machine! But
at least it's better than a maid that speaks
no English.

BEEP. . .

Hi. This is JAN. Maybe you can help me out. My florist is sick—what should I send her?

BEEP. . .

Hi. This is JAN. At the tone, leave a *number*—and if it's *yours*, I'll call you back.

BEEP. . .

Hi. Please leave your name and phone number. I lost my address book and now I don't know who my friends are!

BEEP. . .

Hi. I'm out to lunch. I finally found the consummate diet: you eat until you can't fit through the restaurant door!

BEEP. . .

(GERMAN ACCENT)
You haf reached a *Cherman* answering machine, und you *vill* leaf a message! Ve haf ways of making you talk!

BEEP. . .

Hi. This is JOE. You know, I was just thinking how lucky I am that my name is JOE—'cuz, long as I can remember, that's what people 've been callin' me!

BEEP. . .

*
I'm starry, but the slumber you have breached is not a jerking wonder. Please console your disectory, or cleave a massage at the bone and then clang hup. Tank shoe.

BEEP. . .

(MISCELLANEOUS DIALECT: SPAN-
ISH, AFRO-AMERICAN, SOUTHERN,
BROOKLYN, GERMAN, IRISH, ETC.)

Say what?

BEEP. . .

(The shortest message in the book deserves
a page of its own! C.C.)

CELEBRI-TEASE

Uh, this is the, uh, *William F. Bucklee* Answering Machine Service for JAN. Please impart your cognomen, uh, your telephone integers, and a conservative communiqué at the, uh, sonance of the electronic modulator.

BEEP. . .

Hello. You've reached a *Van Gogh* Answering Machine. There's no limit on the length of your message, so if you want, you can talk my ear off.

BEEP. . .

Hello. This is the *Tony Randill* Answering Service for JOE. Now, when you leave a message, be sure to enunciate clearly, mind your p's and q's, and after you finish, go clean that messy room of yours!

BEEP. . .

Hello. If you leave a message, we'll keep it in the strictest of confidence. You have our word that we will give it to JOE only and no one else! We're the *Benedict Arnold* Answering Service—a name you can trust!

BEEP. . .

(SENSUOUS)
Hi. This is the *Bo Derrik* Answering Machine Service for JAN. Now don't you hang up without leaving your name and number, because I have a *special treat* for caller #10. . .

BEEP. . .

*

Hi. This is *Little Bo Peep*. JAN can't come to the phone right now, she's out trying to find my sheep. When she gets the flock home, I'll tell her to give you a call.

BEEP. . .

Hello. You have reached a *Pavlov* model answering machine. When you hear the sound of the tone you will find yourself subconsciously compelled to leave a message—but watch it so you don't get slobber all over your receiver.

BEEP. . .

Hello. This is the *Hoffa* Answering Service for JOE. Please leave a message and have patience—it may be a while before he calls you back, 'cuz we have no idea where he disappeared to.

BEEP. . .

Hello. This is the *E.F. Huttin* Answering Service for JAN. You know, a lot of callers complain that often they have invested the time to leave a sound message, then never got a decent return call. Well, we're different—when you speak, *E.F. Huttin* listens!

BEEP. . .

Hi. This is the *Bob Dylen* Answering Machine Service for JOE.
How many times must a man check his
    machine,
Before he sees a call?
The answer my friend, is blowing out
    your ear,
The answer is blowing out your ear!

BEEP. . .

*
Hello Americans. This is *Paul Hairvey*.
Page One: Leave your name and number
at the sound of the tone.
Page Two: We will call you back as soon as
possible—and this is a true value.
(PAUSE)
This is *Paul Hairvey*. Good day.

BEEP. . .

(ANGRY)
This is the *Walleye George* Answering
Machine Service for JOE. Either you leave
a good ol' red-blooded, patriotic American
message—or get off the phone! Right now!
I mean it, you commie-pinko-weirdos! Get
outta here!

BEEP. . .

Hello. This is the *Picasso* Answering
Service for JAN.
Message sound tone of—
number name and leave—
call the you time.

BEEP. . .

Hello. This is a *Beethoven* model answering machine. At the tone, leave a message—
but you'll have to speak up!

BEEP. . .

Hello. This is the *Nathan Hale* Answering
Service for JAN. You caught her away
from her phone, but she's bound to be back
very soon, so leave a message and hang
around by your phone.

BEEP. . .

Hi. Please leave a message. You know, I gotta tell ya, I'm kinda proud of my answering machine here. It's a *Pete Ruse* model. Even though it's getting old, slowing down, and has almost outlived its usefulness, it still *manages* to take messages!

BEEP. . .

Hi. Please leave a message. This is the *Roy Roggers* Answering Service for JOE. JOE should be along any minute now. The rest of the *Roy Roggers* crew just got back from lunch and boy are we *stuffed*!

BEEP. . .

MONDAY NIGHT MESSAGE

Hi-yo! This is the *Ed McMann* Answering Service. The answering machine you actually called is off *tonight*. So I'm sort of "Guest Answering." At the tone, leave your name, number and a monologue. Ready? Heeeeeeeeeeeeeeeeerrrrrrrrrrrrrrr's:

BEEP. . .

(GRAND VOICE)
Hello. JAN has graciously allowed me 15 seconds of answering machine time today to use as a forum for a brief public service announcement. . . My name is *Socrates*, and I'm here to warn you about the dangers of drinking. . .

BEEP. . .

This is a *Toulouse-Latrec* model answering machine. At the tone, you only have 20 seconds—so leave a *short* message.

BEEP. . .

This is the *Mr. Whippil* Answering Machine Service for JOE. Now you female callers better not hang up without leaving a message or I'll come over and squeeze your. . .

BEEP. . .

Hello. This is the *Colonel Sandler's* Answering Machine Service for JAN. Now, I realize that answering machines are intimidating, but I can just tell you're not the type who hangs up—'cuz I know a chicken when I hear one!

BEEP. . .

Hello. This is JAN. For your information, you will be leaving your message on a *Dick Clarck* model answering machine. It's as old as the hills, but it looks as good as the day I bought it!

BEEP. . .

Hi. This is the *Annette Funijello* Answering Machine Service for JAN. You know, I really get turned on when a man calls—but not just *any* man—I'm talking, a man with *something extra*! Yeah, I just love men with *great big*. . . ears!

BEEP. . .

This is the *Timothy Leery* Answering Service for JAN. Oh wow! This is really groovy! When you called, this like, really far out message indicator light lit up like the Aurora Borealis! I'm just diggin' on it! It's a truly psychedelic experience! What a rush! Oh, I almost forgot—at the far out tone, please lay some heavy inspiration on us!

BEEP...

This is the *Barnim & Bayley* Answering Machine Service for JOE. Leave a message at the tone and some clown will call you back!

BEEP...

(SEXY FEMALE VOICE)
Hi. This is a *Lony Andersen* model answering machine. If you leave your name and number and don't hang up, I might let you come over sometime and play with my knobs.

BEEP. . .

PHONEY BUSINESS

You have reached the *Equivocation
Society*. This is JAN, the President—
actually, I'm not the president. I'm not
sure what I am, exactly. Anyway, when
you hear the tone—well, it's not really a
tone, it's more of a "beep"—please leave a
message—unless you'd rather leave something else. I don't want you to feel committed—then again, maybe commitment
isn't such a bad idea—on the other hand...

BEEP. . .

Hi. It's *National Answering Machine Safety Week*, and I want to remind you: if you drink, don't leave a message! Have a friend leave it for you. So, at the tone, speak carefully and have a safe phone call!

BEEP. . .

Hello. This is your local *Department of Message Enforcement.* We patrol our city's answering machines daily looking for message violators. If we find that you have illegally hung up, one of our machine-maids will come by and ticket your lips.

BEEP. . .

*

(TV EVANGELIST VOICE)
Greetings, fren's. This is Brother JOE of *The Church of the Perpetual Dialtone.* For low, it is written in the Good Book, upon the Pages which are Yellow, that he who leaveth a message shall have everlasting life, while he who hangeth up shall rot in the Kingdom of Hades for all eternity. So dear fren', secure your salvation and leave a message after the Sacred Tone. A-men.

BEEP. . .

Hello, fellow Americans. This answering machine is sanctioned by the *John Berch Society.* So, when you leave your message, please be sure to speak out of the right side of your mouth. Thank you.

BEEP. . .

You have reached in *IRA Answering Machine*. Have you given any thought to your autumn years when you may no longer be able to produce adequate messages? Well, with this new *IRA Answering Machine*, you can now put away several messages for your retirement. So, at the tone, leave your first deposit. . . Substantial interest penalty for early withdrawal!

BEEP. . .

(SHOUT—AWAY FROM MICROPHONE)
Hello!
This is JAN's *Telethon For The Hard of Hearing*!
At the tone, please your pledge! You hear?

BEEP. . .

*

Hello, and thank you for calling *Heaven*. This is God speaking. I can't answer your call right now, as I'm down in the judgement room deciding who's been good and who's been bad. If you leave your name, number, time of day that you called, and any recent sins you may have committed, I'll get back to you. Once again, thank you for calling *Heaven*, and if you don't leave a message, *you* can go to. . .

BEEP. . .

You reached *Venerable Answering Machine*. Leave message after ancient koan: Confusius say, "man who throw piano in coal mine get *A-flat miner!*"

BEEP. . .

*

(ROBOTIC VOICE)
The *Communication System* at the DOE residence has detected your call. It has come to our attention that certain humans fail to identify themselves to answering devices, instead recording irritating pulse tones into our transducers. What a primative behavior! *Please* I.D. yourself after the beep and leave coordinates where we may contact you to arrange for an encounter. Thank you.
(FEMALE ANNOUNCER VOICE)
This has been a Steven Spillbrain Ultra-Terrestrial Production.

BEEP. . .

*

(FAST)
Hello—this is *JOE's Cemetary*. If you're good you go to Heaven; if you're bad you go to. . . Hello—this is *JOE's Cemetary*. If you're good you go to Heaven; if you're bad you go to. . . Hello—this is *JOE's Cemetary*. If you're good. . .
(ETC.)

BEEP. . .

*

(SOFT MUSIC IN BACKGROUND—
GENTLE VOICE)

Hello, dear friend. You've reached *Dial-A-Prayer*. This is JAN speaking. At the sound of the tone, please leave your prayer-need along with your name and number. I probably can't answer your prayer, but I will answer your call. God bless you.

BEEP. . .

Hi. This is the *Answering Machine Game Show!*
Answer these three questions correctly:
What is your name?
What is your number?
The time you called?
And you will receive an all-expense-paid phone call from JOE!

BEEP. . .

*

(IN BACKGROUND, PLAY: "HEARD IT THROUGH THE GRAPEVINE")
Welcome to *Grapevine Control*, the place to start, confirm or deny a rumor. To give us the *scoop of the day*, get the latest *poop*, or *say it isn't so*, leave your name, number and information at the tone. And remember our motto: "We never repeat gossip. . . so listen closely the first time!"

BEEP. . .

Greetings. This is the *Ghost Society*. If you're a goblin, a poltergeist, an apparition, a spirit, a genie, a phantom, something that goes bump in the night, a gremlin, a banshee, a bogeyman, or your name is Casper, leave a message. But if you claim to be a human, don't bother. Members of the *Ghost Society* don't believe in people!

BEEP. . .

*

You are listening to the *Telecom Answering Device* of Agent (*YOUR PHONE NUMBER*). If you wish a return communication, please wait for the tone, then leave your current identifier, telecom coordinates, optimal communication time and any uncoded communiqués. Over and out!

BEEP. . .

*

(GOOFY VOICE)
Yeah, hi there. You have reached the *Ding-Dong School of Mental Development*, of which I is a graduate. I'm sorry, nobody's here to take your call at dis time, and I can't write nothin' down 'cuz I ain't allowed ta use nothin' with a sharp point. Leave a message and Mr. DOE will call you back. . .
(GOOFY LAUGH)

BEEP. . .

*

Hi. This is *Lotta Hotstuff*. I'm busy now revising my *last* Romance Novel to be published soon as my *new* Romance Novel. If you have anything sensuous, sexy, or even just suggestive to contribute, leave your message after the tone. Happy Romance!

BEEP. . .

(FAST & NERVOUS)
Hi. I'm a *Hypochondriac* model answering machine. Leave a message, but do it quick! I gotta go in the shop again! I've had this nagging pain in my transistors all day—and yesterday my circuits were throbbing like you wouldn't believe! Plus, I'm all out of the special lubrication the repairman gave me last time—not to mention my weak resistors! Oh, and I almost forgot to tell you about my reoccuring. . .

BEEP. . .

*
(SERENE, ETHEREAL VOICE)
Hello and thank you for calling *Father McGuire's "Secret Sins" Theater*. This evening we're showing a French film entitled, "Catholic Cats in Spandex." Do come by and swap sins with the best! Sister Mary JAN signing off!

BEEP. . .

(MOROSE, OR WHINY VOICE)
Hello. You've reached the *Negativity Society*. You can leave a message if you want, but you'll probably be wasting your time. Either we'll accidently erase it, or we'll lose your number, or else we'll just forget to call you back. Actually, I don't know why we even bother to turn this thing on???

BEEP. . .

"INVOLVE"
THE CALLER

(TYPEWRITER CLICKING—ONE KEY)
(NEWS REPORTER VOICE)
Flash: late last night, thieves broke into
the Police Station and stole the toilet—the
cops have nothing to go on!
(PAUSE)
And now, this just in from our Roving
Reporter:

BEEP. . .

(GIRLISH VOICE)
Hi. Guess what? You're my very first caller. Yes, it's true, I'm a *virgin* answering machine. And you're so handsome, so strong, so assertive! I always dreamed my *first message* would be like this! One last thing, please be gentle???

BEEP. . .

Hello. You have reached JAN's *Express* answering machine. As a courtesy to other callers, kindly observe our policy of *ten words or less*! Thank you.

BEEP. . .

*
Hi. This is JAN's answering machine. I'm entered in the Answering Machine Association's *Fewest Hang Ups Contest*. Won't you please help me out and leave a message at the tone? Thanks!

BEEP. . .

(SERIOUS, WORRIED)
Hi. Please don't hang up—I desperately need your advice. Something's been bothering me all day—and I believe you are the *one person* who is qualified to advise me. What I need to know is. . . is there anything good on TV tonight?

BEEP. . .

*
(TO THE TUNE OF "MR. ROGER'S SONG")
It's a beautiful day in the neighborhood,
A beautiful day for a neighbor,
Would you be my,
Could you be my,
Won't you be my neighbor.
The word for today is *Message*.
Can you say *Message*?
(PAUSE)
Now leave one at the beep.

BEEP. . .

Hi. This is JAN. If you're calling to ask me out, leave your name and number and I'll get back—but in the words of Ameilia Erhardt, "I don't go all the way!"

BEEP. . .

*
(FLUSTERED)
Hello? Did I remember to turn this darn answering machine on? If I did, please leave your name and number after the tone. If I didn't, just forget this whole thing!!!

BEEP. . .

Hi. I just got a new "state-of-the-art" answering machine. When you leave your message, I guess you can swear and cuss all you want—it says right here on the box, it's "shock proof".

BEEP. . .

Because of all the controversy surrounding drug abuse in sports, if you're a famous athlete calling, I'm afraid you'll have to submit to a drug test before you can leave a message.
(FAST)
Here's your test: "If four 275 pound linemen split two-and-a-half ounces of pure *Columbian* how many bags of *Cheatos* will they consume?"

BEEP. . .

*

Hello. As JAN's answering machine, I'm here for you to leave any messages, compliments, advice or any other communication you wish at the tone. Please do so as it will make JAN happy with me and maybe she'll raise my allowance. Thank you.

BEEP. . .

*

Hi! Do you know me? Did I leave home without you? Be American. . . *express* yourself. Just leave your name, number and *statement*, and I'll get back to you before your expiration date.

BEEP. . .

Hi. This is JAN. If you have any suggestions of a *good* singles' bar, I'd like to hear them. This place I went to last night was suppose to be a real "meat market". It turned out the "meat" was *turkey*!

BEEP. . .

*

<u>CHRISTMAS MESSAGE</u>

Hello. This is JAN. I can't come to the phone because. . . I'm wrapping *your* Christmas gift. Please leave your name and number so I'll know *whose name* to put on the box!

BEEP. . .

Hi. This is JOE's answering machine. At the tone. . .

Wait a minute, you look a little peaked! Are you feeling alright? I hope it isn't that nasty *Hang Up Disease* that's going around! The only known cure is leaving a message. . .

You don't believe me? Well then, at the tone, give a second opinion!

BEEP. . .

(CLOCK TICKING—5 SECONDS, THEN:)
(EERIE VOICE)
Your eyelids are getting heavy. . . heavier. You are getting sleepy. . . sleepier. And when you hear the tone, you will have a wild desire to leave a message. . .

BEEP. . .

*
(SAD)
They did it again! JAN and JOE have abandoned me—left me alone to phone-sit in this quiet, empty house. JOE even unplugged the electric train, so I have no one to play with. I get so lonely when they leave! Please talk to me at the tone. I could use a human voice right now. Thank you from the bottom of my circuits!

BEEP. . .

Hi. I'll be right back. I just ran down to the corner store to get a diet drink. Tell me, what do you think: if a person was going to try to lose a hundred pounds in a week, would you say he had a fat chance—or a slim chance?

BEEP. . .

Hi. I'm not home. My boyfriend invited me over for dinner. He tries so hard to please, and I hate to hurt his feelings, but how do I tell him, you don't boil *meatloaf*?!?

BEEP. . .

*

HALLOWEEN MESSAGE

(ORGAN IN BACKGROUND)
(WITCH'S VOICE)
Boil and bubble, bubble and boil. Heh, heh, heh. We're busy cooking up some treats for Halloween. Eye of newt, toe of frog, wool of bat and tongue of dog. Enough gourmet food. I'm sure your mouth is watering, but this stuff needs constant stirring. So if you leave your name and message, I'll see that you get invited to dinner. Heh, heh, heh.

BEEP. . .

(FRUSTRATED)

Hi. I can't come to the phone—I'm trying to balance my checkbook!!! Can anybody tell me why is it that at the end of the money, there is still so much of the month left over???

BEEP. . .

Yes I want you to leave a message at the tone. . .
Yes I miss you. . .
Yes I wish you were here. . .
Yes I have so many things to say to you— so many things to share—whoever the heck you are. . .

BEEP. . .

Warning: This machine has been specially wired by the Police Department to help capture the *Hang Up Bandit*—and you're a suspect! So leave a message—but don't leave town!

BEEP. . .

(TALK INTO CUPPED HANDS)
Okay, we're about ready to tape the answering machine message to JOE. Let's have it quiet on the set! Okay, we got the *star* on the phone ready to leave a message at the tone. Okay, now remember to deliver your lines with *feeling*! Ready? Okay, lights. . . tape's rolling. . . and. . . *action*!

BEEP. . .

This is JAN with your chance to be *Tarmac the Magnificent*!
The answer is. . .
"The Thanksgiving Bird, the country next to Greece, and *you* if you hang up!"
(TEAR OPEN ENVELOPE)
And the question is. . .

BEEP. . .

MISSING:

LAST SEEN
APRIL 1, 1986

CHAPTERLESS
MESSAGES

Hi. This is JOE. I'll be right back. I just
went down to the liquor store. By the way,
have you heard the latest? They're gonna
put pictures of missing husbands on beer
cans.

BEEP. . .

(FRUSTRATED)
Hi. I was going to ask you to do something but now I don't remember what it was??? Something about leaving something at the sound of something else??? It makes me mad I can't think of what it was—and what's this lump doing on my head???

BEEP. . .

*

Hi. This is JAN. I can't come to the phone right now because:
A: I'm not home.
B: I'm outside.
Or **C:** I'm having sex.
Mom, if it's you calling, it's not **C**!

BEEP. . .

*

Hi. JOE can't come to the phone right now
'cuz he's in the kitchen raiding the frig.
He'll call you back. . .
(MUNCH, MUNCH)
when he's through with his mouth-water-
ing. . .
(MUNCH, MUNCH)
baloney sandwich. You see, if he talked to
you now, you'd just get a lot of *phoney
baloney*!

BEEP. . .

*

(INTELLECTUAL VOICE)
I'm not home right now, so leave a message. However, when promulgating your
esoteric cogitations, beware of the plati-
tudinous of jejune babblements! Oh, I'm
sorry. . . just don't use big words, okay?

BEEP. . .

Hi. I've gone out to a movie—hope it's better than the one I saw yesterday. This movie that premiered last night was so bad, when I got home it was already on cable!

BEEP. . .

Hi. This is JAN with a special announcement: Will the person who called about the *Memory Course* please call back! I forgot what I did with your number!

BEEP. . .

*
Merry Christmas. JOE and JAN are not at home right now. Leave your name and number and they will call you back.
(LOUDLY AND OFF TO THE SIDE)
Hey, little fat man. I don't care who you are. You and your reindeer get off my roof!

BEEP. . .

SPECIAL SMOKER'S SECTION

(BAD SMOKER'S COUGH)
Hi. At the tone, leave a message.
(COUGH-COUGH)
Please excuse me! Darn! This time I'm determined to do something!
(COUGH-COUGH)
Lately I've read a lot of really scary stuff about the bad effects of smoking, so I've made up my mind to quit. . .
(COUGH-COUGH)
reading!

BEEP. . .

(None of the other messages would consent to share this page. C.C.)

*
(TO THE TUNE OF "WE ARE THE WORLD")
We are the tape, you are the message.
You have a chance to brighten up our day,
So don't be selfish.
Don't hang up the phone,
When hear the beep say "hi".
It's true we make a better tape,
Just you and I.

BEEP. . .

THANKSGIVING

Happy Thanksgiving! We're out in the yard with all the relatives. Feel free to come by if you want. We still have plenty of leftover turkey—from last year!

BEEP. . .

*

Hello. This is JOE. I think I'm on the verge of a great scientific discovery! You know when you do your laundry, how you're always missing one sock? Well, I think I discovered what happens to them— they become clothes hangers in your closet. I'm always finding extra ones!

BEEP. . .

Hi. This is JOE. I'm on vacation. But I've got one of those machines where you can change your outgoing message by remote. . .
(PAUSE—SLIGHT PANIC)
Oh shoot! If I'm not mistaken, I think I took off and forgot to lock my house!!!
(PAUSE—RELAXED)
But, then again, I also forgot to feed my Dobermans. . .

BEEP. . .

77

Hi. I went over to my Aunt and Uncle's. They're complainers, so I'll only stay a half-hour. On the way back I gotta stop by my boring cousin's, but only for a minute. Then I'll drop in and say an obligatory "hi" to my fussy neice. So leave a message and I'll get back to you *relatively* soon.

BEEP. . .

(SERIOUS & CONFIDENTIAL)
Hello. This is just between you and me, but I thought you should know certain privileged information that heretofore, only I have access to. For example, there are literally millions of Martians secretly living among us. As I speak, the Russians have thousands of nuclear submarines hidden along our country's entire coastline, and the CIA is monitoring every move we make.
(CHEERY)
Well, gotta go. My bath is ready.

BEEP. . .

Hi. I'm at my psychiatrist's. I have to say the guy's accomodating—he just bought a new piece of office furniture for his schizophrenic patients: bunk beds.

BEEP. . .

Hi. This is JOE. I'm feeling great today and I want to take this opportunity to thank each and every one of my friends—'cuz without all of you, I'd be a total stranger!

BEEP. . .

(ECHO EFFECT)
Hello— hello. . .
This is JOE— Joe. . .
I hadda go to the dentist— dentist. . .
I've got a great big cavity— cavity. . .

BEEP. . .

Hi. I'm not in. I'm going over to Grandpa's today. You know, I wish he'd act his age. I don't mind him popping his bubble gum, or the beanie he wears, but the baseball cards flapping in his wheelchair spokes are a little too much!

BEEP. . .

*
(OVEN-TIMER TICKING)
TIC-TIC-TIC-TIC-TIC-TIC-TIC-TIC. . .
(SERIOUS VOICE)
Time is running out. . .
If you want to leave a message. . .
You better do it soon. . .
TIC-TIC-TIC-TIC-TIC-TIC-TIC-TIC. . .

BEEP. . .

*
Please pity my poor virgin machine,
Whose messages are mostly obscene.
So just speak after the beep,
Nothing sordid or cheap,
And I'll return all the calls that are clean!

BEEP...

(UNEMOTIONAL)
Sorry if you weren't able to reach me the last couple of weeks, but I was on vacation. I went to the Midwest. All my friends said it would probably be *boring*—but let me tell you, I had a time there. For example, one day I went out and after that I came back. Also, there were some places to visit, so I drove over and sure enough, they were there. All in all, it certainly was, and I'm thinking, next year—who knows?

BEEP...

*
(CAPTAIN KIRK VOICE)
Tape. . . the final frontier. These are the messages of JOE and JAN's answering machine, its five second mission, to seek out your name and telephone number. To boldly record what no machine has recorded before!

BEEP. . .

You know, there must be 50 ways to leave a message. . .
Just call me back, Jack—
Tell me your plan, Stan—
You don't need a ploy, Roy—
Just call on me.

Give me a buzz, Gus—
You don't have to discuss much—
Just say something brief, Leif—
And you'll be hearin' from me!

BEEP. . .

(EXCITED)
Hi! This is my new answering machine!
Boy did I get a great deal on it! You won't
believe what I paid! Incredible deal! I
don't see how they can possibly sell these
machines for only
(DRAW OUT WORDS)
T e e e e e e e e e n n n n n n n n
b u u u u u u u u c c c c c c c k s !

BEEP. . .

(FAST)
Hello. You've reached *PHONE NUMBER*.
I just left for the office. The number there
is *PHONE NUMBER*. If you need to get in
touch with me right away, halfway between here and the office is a phone
booth—let's see, I think the number is. . .

BEEP. . .

Hi. Leave a message at the beep. . .
(PAUSE—FRUSTRATED)
Now where'd I put that beep???
(OPEN AND CLOSE 2 OR 3 DRAWERS)
Not there. . . Not there. . .
(RELIEVED)
Ah, here it is. . .

BEEP. . .

5. Contest begins July 1, 1986. Entries must be postmarked by March 31, 1987. Winners will be selected on April 30, 1987 and notified by mail within 15 days. Entry constitutes permission to use winners' names and likenesses for promotional purposes. Additionally, winners may be required to sign and return an affidavit of eligibility and a release within 30 days of notification, for publicity purposes without further compensation, otherwise alternate winners may be selected.

6. Limit: one major prize per family or household. Employees of CCC Publications, their families, agencies and representatives are not eligible. No substitutions for prizes offered. Tax liability to be borne solely by the winners.

7. CCC Publications shall not be liable for late, misdirected, lost or stolen entries.

8. For a list of major prize winners, send a **separate** stamped and self-addressed envelope to "Best Message" Winners List, CCC Publications, 20306 Tau Place, Chatsworth, CA 91311.

9. In the event CCC Publications decides to use a non-winning message, after contest closing, in a future book, you will receive $5 and your name will appear in said book.

ALL PRIZES GUARANTEED TO BE AWARDED